Even More

PRACTICAL TOPICS

FOR THE

EARLY YEARS

GW01319420

Janet Adams

Introduction

Following the success of the previous two books in this series Janet Adams has written "Even More Practical Topics for the Early Years". All three books provide **PHOTOCOPIABLE** tried and tested practical ideas for use in Playgroup, Nursery and Reception classes. The sixty four pages of activities cover the themes: Something Fishy, Houses and Homes, Creepy Crawlies and Looking After Myself. Each activity includes: a concept to explore, a photocopiable outline, something to make, a rhyme to learn, a follow up activity and suggestions for discussion.

Topical Resources publishes a range of Educational Materials for use in Primary School and Pre-School Nurseries and Playgroups.
For latest catalogue:

Tel: 01772 863158 or
Fax: 01772 866153 or

E.Mail: sales@topical-resources.co.uk
Visit our Website on:
www.topical-resources.co.uk

Acknowledgements:
For permission to reprint Copyright material the Editor is indebted to:
Elizabeth Matherson for the following poems published in the 1969 edition of "This Little Puffin" - Puffin Books -
Here is the sea, the Wavy sea.
This is my little house.
Incy Wincy Spider climbed up the water spout.

Heather Bell for -
Fishing in the water.
I'm a little fish.
I'm a little caterpillar.

The publishers have endeavoured to trace the copyright holders of all rhymes used in this publication. If we have unwittingly infringed copyright, we sincerely apologise, and will be pleased, on being satisfied as to the owner's title, to pay an appropriate fee as if we had been able to obtain prior permission.

Copyright © 1999 Janet Adams
Illustrated by Paul Sealey
Printed in Great Britain for "Topical Resources", Publishers of Educational Materials, PO. Box 329, Broughton, Preston, England. PR3 5LT by T.Snape & Co.Ltd., Boltons Court, Preston, England. PR1 3TY

Typeset by Paul Sealey Illustration and Design, 3 Wentworth Drive, Thornton, England. FY5 5AR.
First Published May 1999
ISBN 1-872977-42-1

Contents

© **Topical Resources.** May be photocopied for classroom use only.

Something Fishy

3

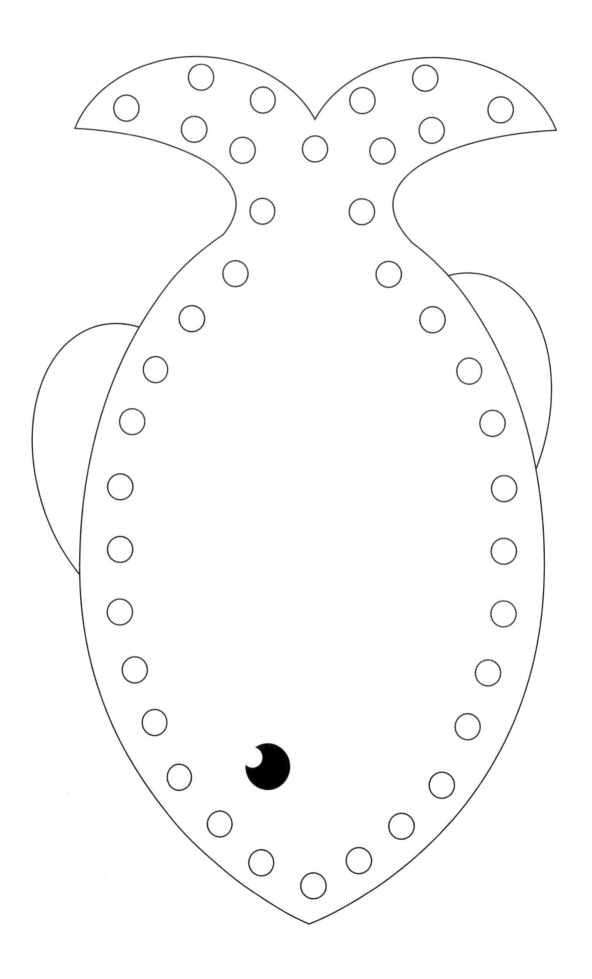

4

© **Topical Resources.** May be photocopied for classroom use only.

A Threaded Fish

Make: A Threaded Fish

Card, blunt large eyed needle, wool / raffia etc. sequins.
1.   Copy the fish onto brightly coloured card and cut out the shape.
2.   Punch out an even number of holes around the edge.
3.   Thread with brightly coloured wool, raffia etc.
4.   Draw on an eye and decorate with sequins.

This can be part of a large undersea display.

Rhyme: Fishing in the water,
What will there be?
Pull up my hook,
And what do I see?
A little silver fishy,
Just looking up at me!

(Heather Bell)

Activity: Use the shape opposite as a template. Cut fish shapes out of magazines using any sort of pictures to create abstract patterned fish. Stick onto plain blue paper with a fluted top edge to look like the surface of the water.

Talk About: Look at books and pictures of fishes.
Look at different shapes, sizes, colours and patterns.

6

© **Topical Resources.** May be photocopied for classroom use only.

Underwater Picture

Make: <u>An 'Exploded' Underwater Picture</u>

Blue activity paper, shades of green activity paper, assorted coloured / textured papers, glue, scissors, card.

1.   Make card templates of the shapes opposite.
2.   Cut out as many fish and seaweed shapes, using the templates, as appropriate to the child's ability.
3.   Carefully cut each of the shapes into four or five pieces using wavy or zig-zag lines.
4.   Place the pieces of each shape carefully onto a large sheet of blue paper, like jigsaws, but leaving spaces between each piece so that the blue appears to make stripes in each fish and piece of seaweed. Stick down.

Rhyme: Here is the sea, the wavy sea.
Here is the boat and here is me,
All the fishes down below
Wiggle their tails and away they go!
(This Little Puffin)

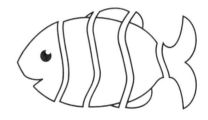

Activity: Using the same templates cut out one large fish and three small fishes. Colour with felt pens and make a picture to illustrate the song "Down in the river in an iddy piddy pool, lives three little fishes and a mommy fish too..." - or use a similar "fishy" song.

Talk About: The different places where fish can live e.g. rivers, ponds, the seas. How we can take care of the fish's environment.

© **Topical Resources.** May be photocopied for classroom use only.

Shells in a Bucket

Make: <u>Shells in a Bucket</u>

A selection of different kinds of shells, paper, margarine tubs, card.

1. Make a bucket out of a margarine tub. The tub can be painted / covered with paper / covered with aluminium foil. Fix a card handle on to the sides of the tub.
2. Let each child choose four or five different shells. Draw round the shells on a suitable sized piece of paper.
3. On the top of the paper write "I can match these shells".
4. Put the shells in the bucket. Can the child match the drawn shapes with the real shells?

Rhyme: A tongue twister -
Sally sells sea shells on the sea shore.
Change the name if there is a child whose name begins with 'S'.
Five fat fish fight for food etc.

Activity: Photocopy the sheet opposite, talk about the pictures, count and colour.

Talk About: Shells. Look at a collection of shells.
Sort them out.
Look at their shapes, colours, sizes.
Use shells for counting activities.

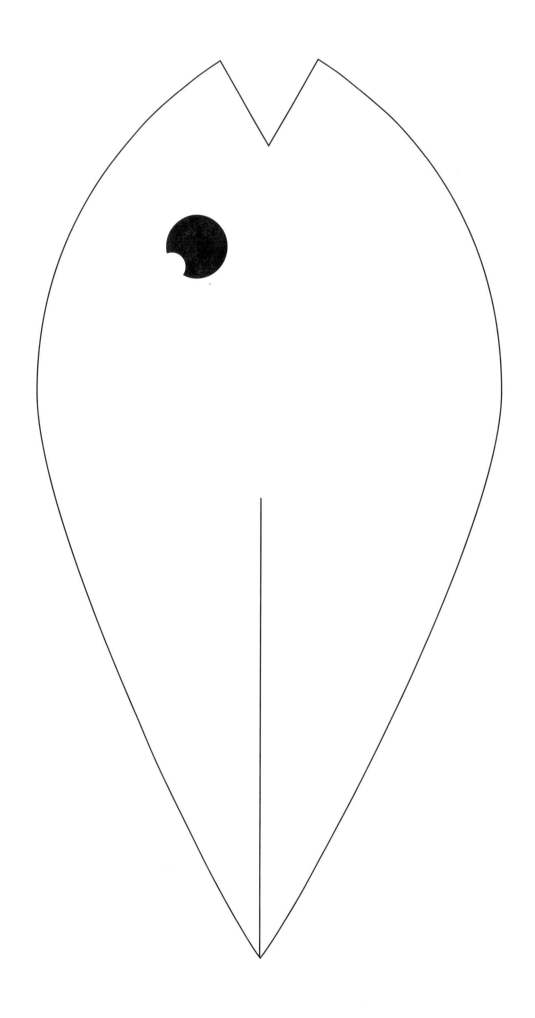

© **Topical Resources.** May be photocopied for classroom use only.

A Fish on a Line

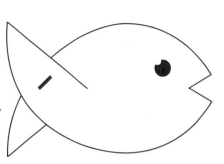

Make: **A Fish on a Line**

Card, scissors, stapler, crayons, cotton, straws.

1.   Copy and cut out the fish opposite using card.
2.   Colour on both sides with crayon.
3.   Cut along the line in the middle.
4.   Cross over the two sides of the cut and staple to make a tail.
5.   Thread a length of cotton from the top of the fish's back and tie on to a drinking straw to look like a fish on a line.

Rhyme: 1, 2, 3, 4, 5,
Once I caught a fish alive.
6, 7, 8, 9, 10,
Then I let it go again.
Why did you let it go?
Because it bit my finger so.
Which finger did it bite?
This little finger on my right.

(Traditional)

Activity: Make an aquarium using a cereal box cut into two. Colour the inside blue or line with blue tissue paper covered with glue. Put glue on to base and cover with sand. Make some fishes out of card and suspend from the top. Add seaweed, pebbles, etc.

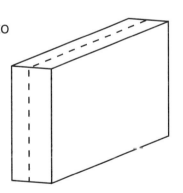

Talk About: The parts of a fish e.g. scales, gills, tail, eyes.
Look at live fish in a fish tank or aquarium, a fish from a fish mongers etc.
Touch the scales.

small
fish

place on fold

small
fish bowl

large fish

large fish bowl

© **Topical Resources.** May be photocopied for classroom use only.

A Fish in a Bowl

Make: <u>A Fish in a Bowl</u>

Blue paint, washing up liquid, straws, plastic containers, milk bottle tops / gold or silver paper, P.V.A. glue.

1.   Using the shapes opposite, cut out a large fish bowl.
2.   Mix some blue paint with a little washing up liquid in a plastic water pot.
3.   Use a straw and blow bubbles until they reach the top of the pot.
4.   Place the bowl shape sheet of paper on top of the coloured bubbles made. Bubble print all over the fish bowl shape.
5.   Cut out the large fish in any colour of paper.
6.   Cover the fish with bottle tops, using P.V.A. glue - over lap a little to look like scales.

Small gold or silver circles can be used instead with sequins, buttons etc.

Rhyme: Swimming round my fish bowl,
Makes you think I'm busy.
But all it makes me really feel,
Is very, very dizzy!
(Janet Adams)

Activity: Cut out the small fish bowl in black paper and several small fishes in luminous paper. Stick fishes on bowl and draw bubbles from the mouths using white or silver crayons. Build display as a counting picture.
e.g. 1 fish and 1 bubble, 2 fishes with 2 bubbles etc.

Talk About: Look at a real fish in a bowl.
How does it move? Does it keep still? Does it stay in one part of the bowl? Does it move to the surface? Observe it eating.

© **Topical Resources.** May be photocopied for classroom use only.

Matching Game

Make: <u>**A Seaside Matching Game**</u>

Card, crayon, scissors

1. Photocopy the picture opposite on to card. (Can be enlarged to A3).
2. Colour each pair of pictures the same - so that they match.
3. Cut out carefully along the lines.

Each child can play a game by themselves and then with a partner. Place all the pictures faced down. Turn over one card, turn over another - if they match keep them out, if they don't then turn them back again. These cards could also be used for snap or laminated and adapted to a lotto game.

Rhyme: I'm a little fish,
Under the sea,
The great blue boat.
Sails over me.
Deep in the sea weed,
There I stay.
Little boy catching fish,
I swim away.

(Heather Bell)

Activity: Photocopy the following three sheets. Cut each sheet into two to make six pages. Staple together to make a Dot - to - Dot Seaside Book.

Talk About: Use the dot - to - dot book illustrations to talk about things we play with at the seaside.
Protecting ourselves from the sun.
Clothes for the seaside.
Natural features and creatures.

My Dot-to-Dot Seaside Book

by _____

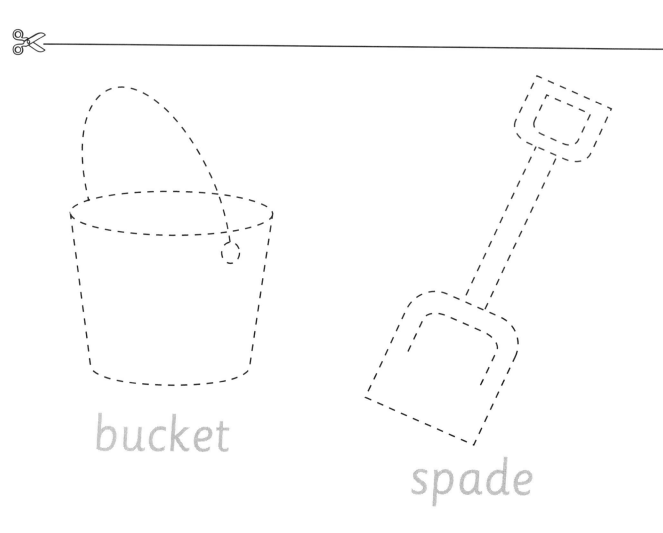

bucket

spade

© **Topical Resources.** May be photocopied for classroom use only.

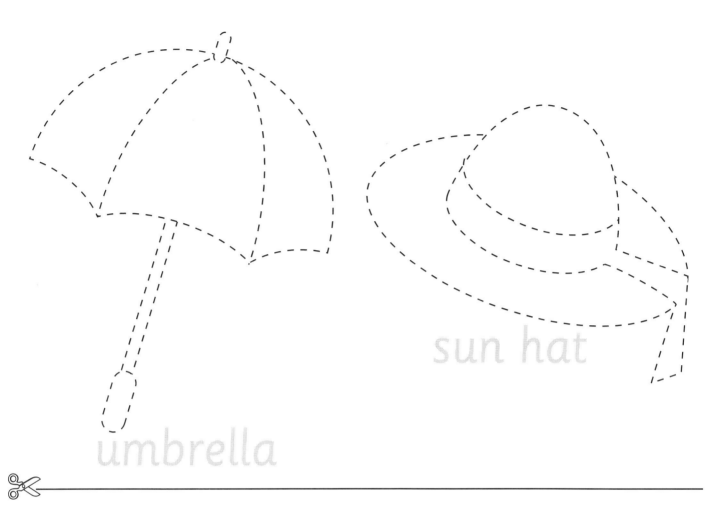

sun hat

umbrella

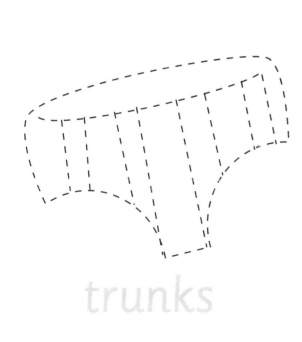

trunks

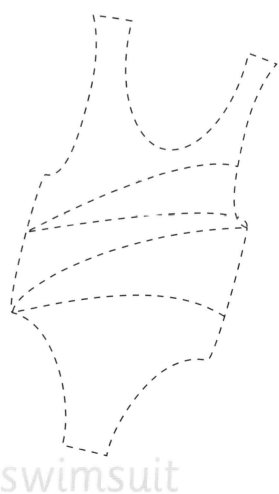

swimsuit

© **Topical Resources.** May be photocopied for classroom use only.

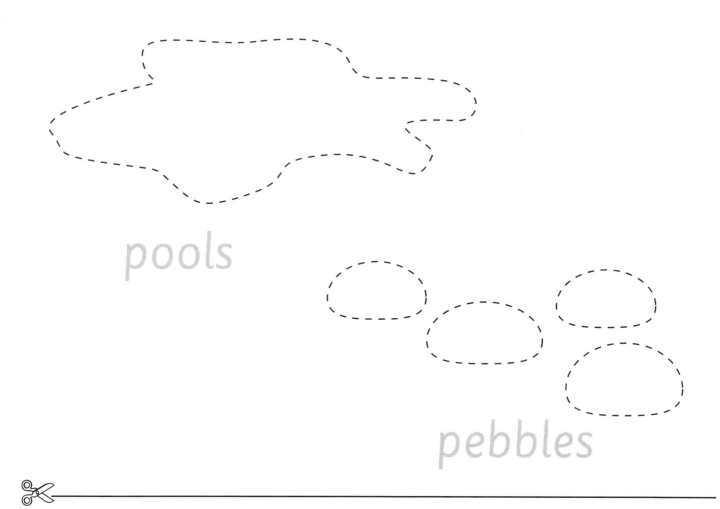

pools

pebbles

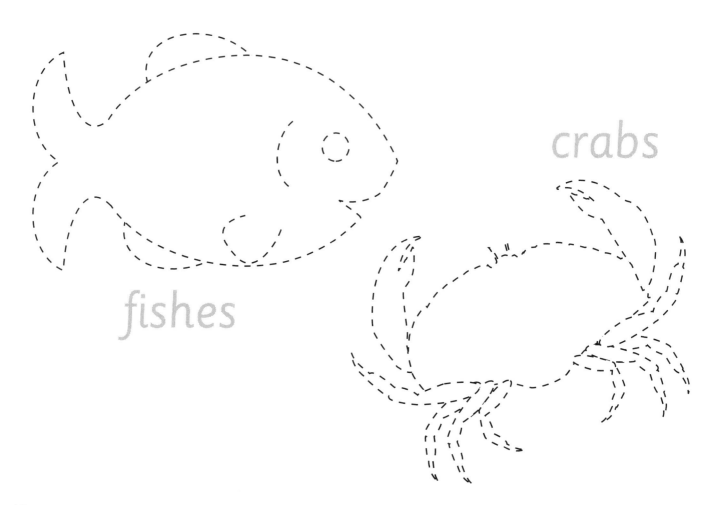

crabs

fishes

18

© **Topical Resources.** May be photocopied for classroom use only.

Houses and Homes

© **Topical Resources.** May be photocopied for classroom use only.

Matching Houses

Make: <u>Matching Houses</u>

Paper, pencils, crayons

1. Photocopy the sheet opposite.
2. Draw lines to match the different types of houses. Colour each pair the same.
   Other uses for this sheet could be:
   a. Comparing the different types of houses.
   b. Counting how many windows each bungalow has, each house etc.
   c. Colouring - e.g. all the chimney pots black, all the windows in the flats blue etc.
   d. Recognise the different numbers on the doors.

Rhyme: Some houses are joined together,
Some houses are all alone.
Whatever the shape and size of my house,
It will always be my home.

(Janet Adams)

Activity: Let each child paint a picture of their own house. When dry go round the outline with thick black felt pen and cut out. Stick all the houses onto a long frieze. Write the title. "This is Where I live". Other pictures can be added e.g. ourselves, cats, dogs, cars, trees, vehicles etc.

Talk About: If possible collect some large photographs / pictures from magazines of houses.
Talk about those with / without an upstairs, bungalows / houses / terraced / detached / semi-detached / flats etc.
Make a simple graph or chart of our houses.

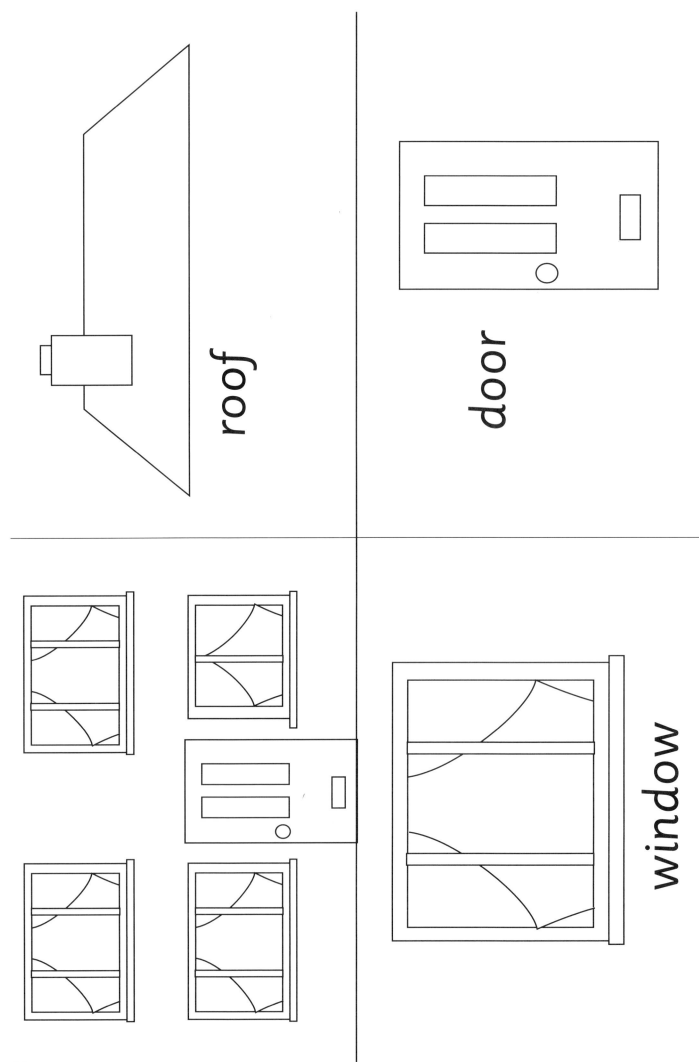

roof

door

window

© **Topical Resources.** May be photocopied for classroom use only.

A House Book

Make: **A House Book**

Paper, crayons, scissors

1.   Photocopy the sheet opposite.
2.   Carefully fold into quarters and cut into four pages.
3.   Put the picture of the house front first, then assemble the other three
      pages behind.
4.   Staple together at the left hand side to make a little book.
5.   Make a separate roof and stick onto the front page.
6.   To make a more textured effect put the front page on top of a rough
      surface and shade with a wax crayon (i.e. wax rubbing).
7.   Colour the door, windows, curtains and roof to match the front cover.

Rhyme: This is my little house, this is the door.
                  The windows are shining, and so is the floor.
                  Outside there is a chimney, as tall as can be.
                  With smoke that goes curling up - come and see.
                  (This Little Puffin)

Activity: Cover a cereal box with plain paper / wood chip paper. Paint windows and
                  doors on the box. Make a simple roof either by folding a strip of card
                  lengthways and resting it on top of the box or fold a strip twice to make a
                  more rigid triangular shape and stick down on top of the box. e.g.

Talk About: Make a set of flash cards - house, roof, window, door.
                  Match the cards to a large picture of a house.
                  Match the words to those in the books and models.

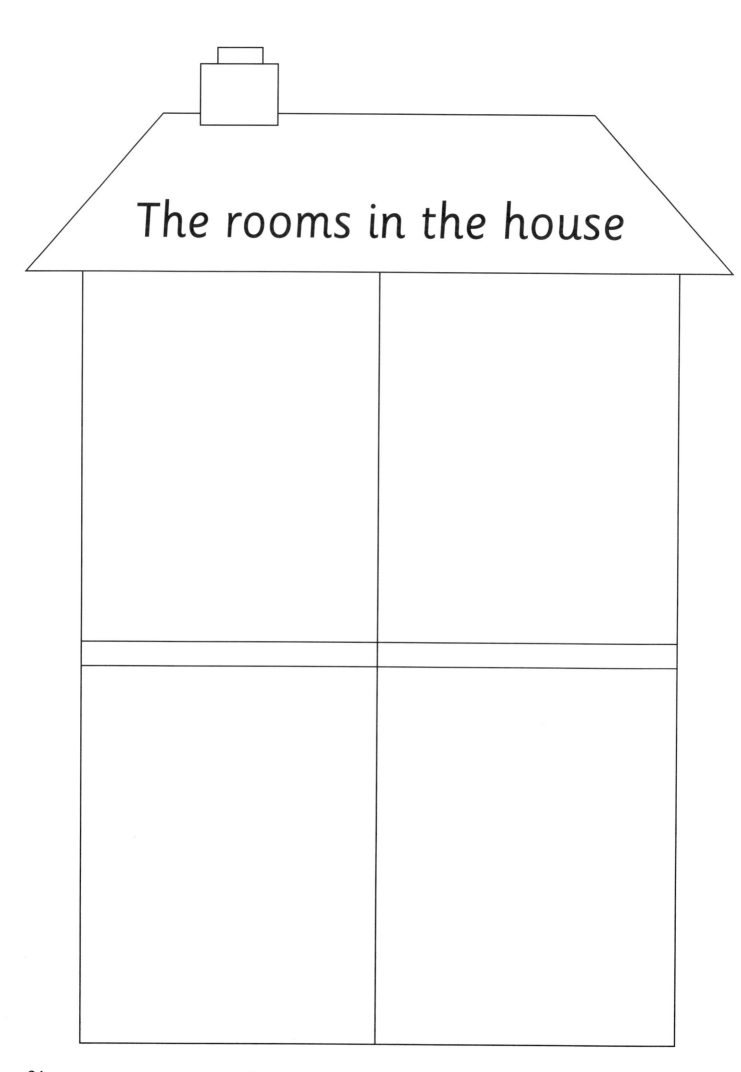

The rooms in the house

© **Topical Resources.** May be photocopied for classroom use only.

Rooms in the House

Make: <u>Rooms in the House</u>

Old magazines / catalogues, scissors, glue.

1. Enlarge the picture opposite.
2. Name each room as the child wishes e.g. bathroom, bedroom / my bedroom, kitchen, dining room, sitting room, playroom etc.
3. Let s/he cut out pictures from catalogues of furniture etc. for each room and stick them on the picture.

Rhyme: Make own rhyme using rhythm of "Granny's in the kitchen". Using children's own ideas e.g.
Mummy's in the kitchen doing a bit of cooking, how many cookers can you count? One!
James is in the sitting room playing with his lego, how many blue bricks can you count? Two!
Peter's in the bathroom doing a bit of splashing, how many sponges can you count? Three!
etc.

Activity: On a long sheet of paper write: "Things we use at home". Divide the paper into the members of each child's family e.g. Mummy, Daddy, Clare, John, Me. Find pictures in magazines etc. of some of the things used by each member of the family and stick under the correct person's name.

Talk About: The different rooms in a house and their names and furnishings.
Make up games e.g. Divide the children into four groups e.g. sitting room, kitchen, bathroom, bedroom. Name four corners of the room the same. Hold up a picture e.g. a fridge, the kitchen. Children run to the kitchen corner.

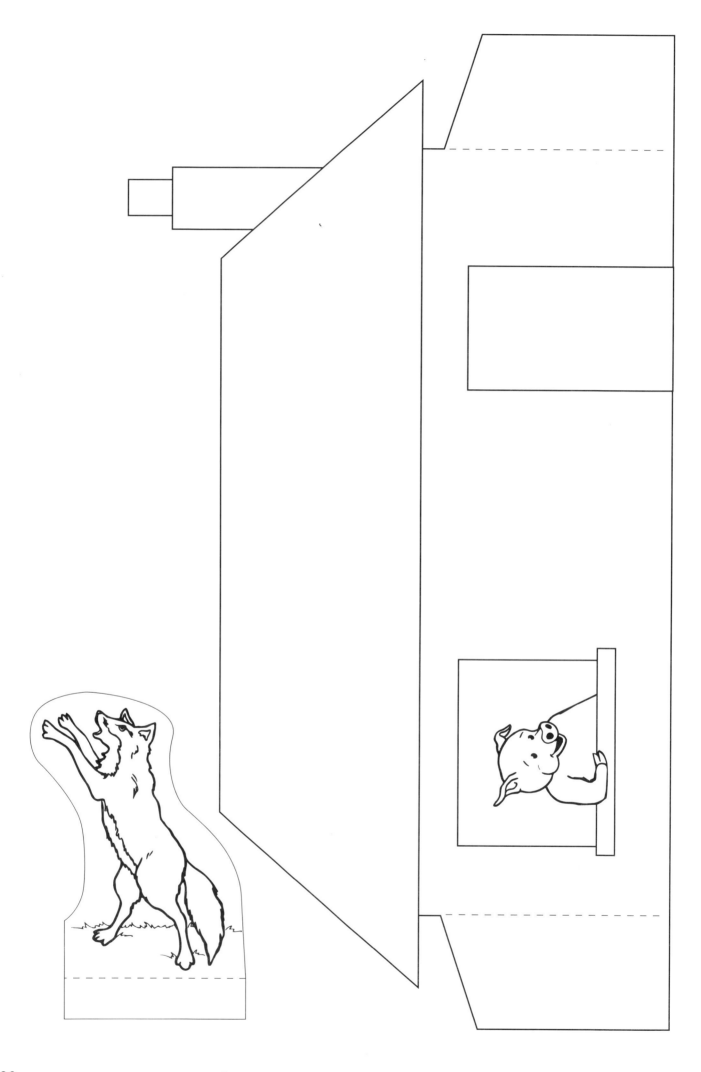

26

© **Topical Resources.** May be photocopied for classroom use only.

The Three Little Pigs

Make: **<u>The Homes of the Three Little Pigs</u>**

Card, thick card, wood shavings/ sticks/ match sticks, straw/ hay/ dried grass, paper, small building bricks, red paint, P.V.A. glue, activity paper, scissors.

1. Make a template of the house opposite.
2. Cut out three houses in thick card and fold back the flaps to make them stand up.
3. Stick onto each one materials which are appropriate to the story e.g. (1) - wood, (2) - straw, (3) - cover with paper (woodchip gives a good surface) and print with a small building brick to look like a brick wall.
4. Stick the three houses onto a long piece of paper.
5. Colour the pig's face in each window.
6. Cut out the wolf and fold back the flap to make him stand. Colour and stand by the first house.

Alternatively the houses could be covered on both sides and turned into a mobile.

Rhyme: 1. The first pig made his house of wood, (3 times)
And the wolf knocked on his door.
The wolf went huff and the wolf went puff, (3 times)
And he blew the house right down.
2. The second pig made his house of straw, etc.
3. The third pig made his house of bricks, etc.
But he could not blow it down.

(Janet Adams)

Activity: Divide a piece of paper into four. Think of four different building materials e.g. wood, brick, glass, metal. Find pictures in magazines where the different materials have been used. Cut out and stick onto the correct quarter.

Talk About: The materials used in the building of a house. Look at samples of building materials. If appropriate visit a small building site.
Talk about why some materials are used for certain things. Why for example aren't walls made of glass, window panes of metal etc.

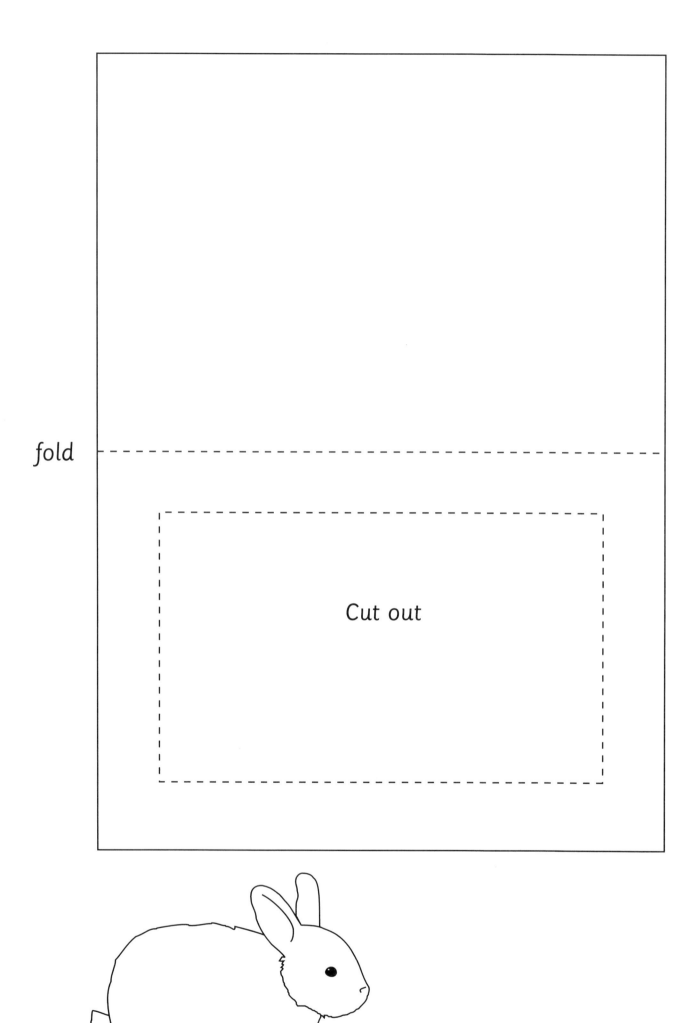

fold

Cut out

28

© **Topical Resources.** May be photocopied for classroom use only.

A Rabbit in a Hutch

Make: **A Rabbit in a Hutch**

Card, crayons / felt pens, scissors, plastic mesh e.g. from vegetable bags.

1.   Make a template of the hutch. Cut out from brown card or colour it brown.
2.   Cut out a section of the hutch as shown.
3.   Stick / tape / staple a rectangle of mesh from behind the space.
4.   Stick a strip of card to the inside of the hutch for the rabbit to be secured to.
5.   Cut out the rabbit shape. Colour / paint or print using a sponge or make own vegetable printing block.
6.   Fix the rabbit to the card spine.
7.   Stand up the completed hutch.
       This idea could also be used for an Easter Card.

Rhyme: A hutch is home for a rabbit,
                A kennel is home for a dog.
                A sty is the home for a pig,
                And a pond is home for a frog!
                (Janet Adams)

Activity: Photocopy the following two pages. Cut each sheet into three to make six pages. Staple together to make an Animal Homes Book.

Talk About: Fairy stories with houses in them e.g. Hansel and Gretal, Goldilocks, Little Red Riding Hood etc.
                Act out the stories.
                What would the houses have been like?

My Animal Homes Book

by _____

a pig lives in a sty

– – –   – – –

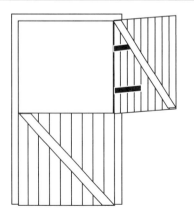

a horse lives in a stable

– – – – – – – – – –

30

© **Topical Resources.** May be photocopied for classroom use only.

a dog lives in a kennel

 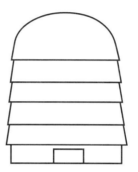

a bee lives in a hive

a bird lives in a nest

© Topical Resources. May be photocopied for classroom use only.

32

© **Topical Resources.** May be photocopied for classroom use only.

A Counting House

Make: <u>A Counting House</u>

Paper, crayons

Photocopy the sheet opposite. The picture can be coloured.
The picture has the following number of features:

      1 chimney and 1 chimney pot

      2 roofs

      3 doors

      4 panes in each window in the house

      5 windows in the house

      6 panes in each window in the garage

      7 Windows altogether

      8 clouds in the sky

Match the number of features to the numbers at the bottom of the sheet by drawing lines with coloured crayons. Use the sheet on the next page to accompany the activity.

Rhyme: Look at the house,
What can you see?
How many chimneys (doors, window etc.)
Can you count for me?

(Janet Adams)

Activity: Use commercially produced gummed or self adhesive geometric shapes to make a picture of a house. Learn the names of the shapes as well as counting them.

Talk About: If possible go outside and look at houses.
Count chimneys. Look at shapes of window panes.
How are the houses different.
Look for numbers on doors, gates etc.

Look at the picture
Fill in the missing numbers

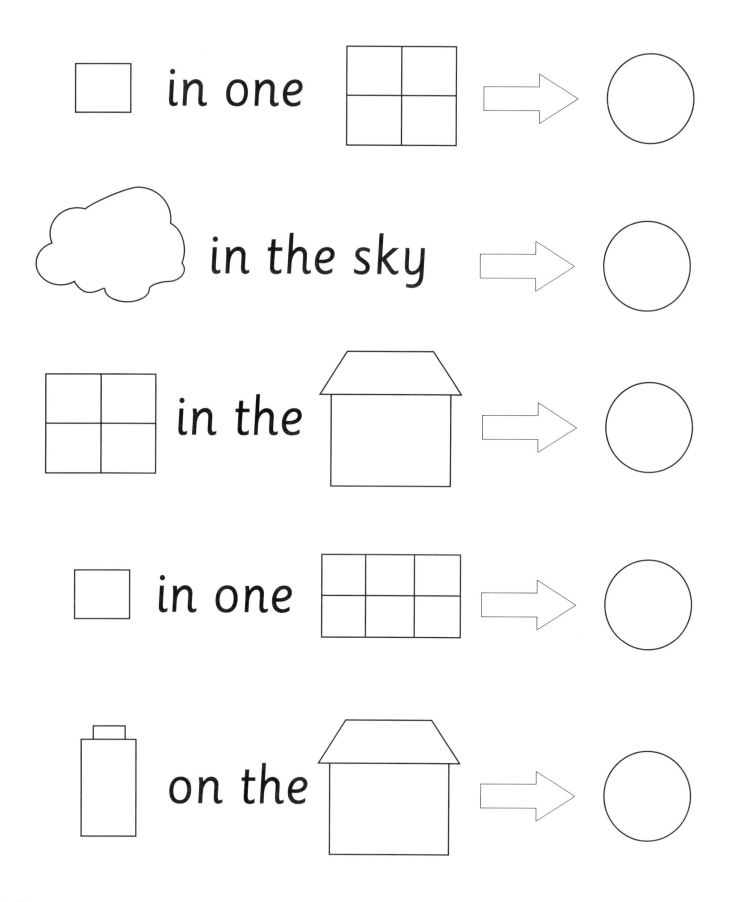

☐ in one → ◯

in the sky → ◯

in the → ◯

☐ in one → ◯

on the → ◯

© Topical Resources. May be photocopied for classroom use only.

Creepy Crawlies

Incy Wincy Spider

© **Topical Resources.** May be photocopied for classroom use only.

Incy Wincy Spider

Make: <u>**Incy Wincy Spider**</u>

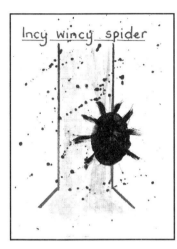

Paper, grey / brown crayon, small potatoes, blue and black paint

1. Photocopy the sheet opposite.
2. Colour the drain pipe either grey or brown.
3. Print the body of the spider climbing up the spout with half a small potato using black paint.
4. Paint some legs onto the spider's body.
5. Flick blue paint over the whole picture to represent the rain.

Rhyme: Incy Wincy spider climbed up the water spout,
Down came the raindrops and washed poor Incy out.
Out came the sunshine and dried up all the rain,
And Incy Wincy spider climbed up that spout again.

(This Little Puffin)

Activity: Use the same background sheet and make four different pictures to shown four lines of the song. They can be used for sequencing.

Talk About: Find more finger rhymes about insects e.g. "What do you suppose, a bee sat on my nose!"
Find stories to talk about and act out.

A Spider's Web

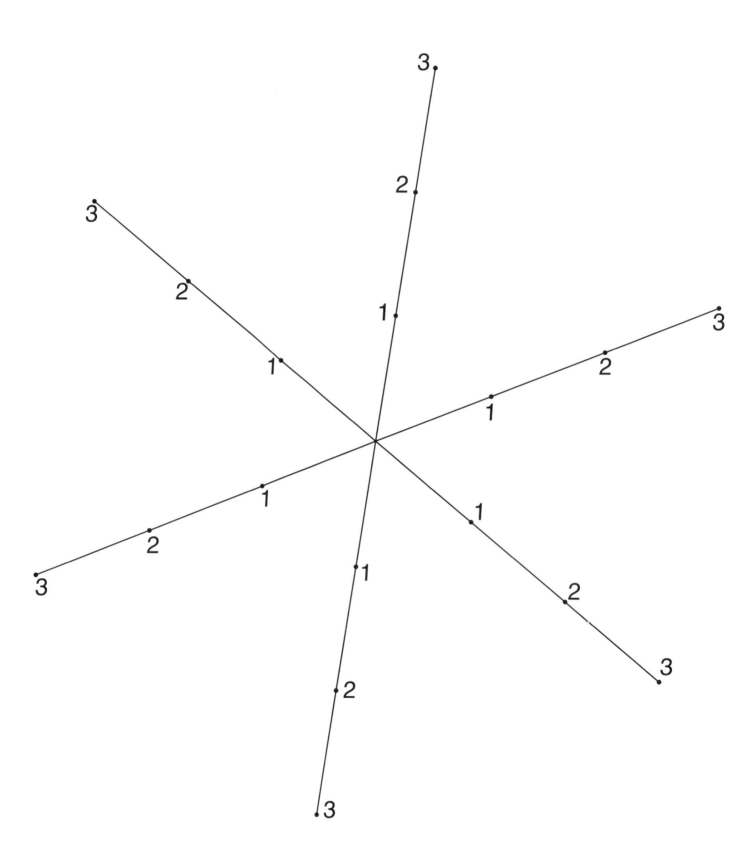

 © **Topical Resources.** May be photocopied for classroom use only.

A Spider's Web

Make: <u>A Spider's Web</u>

Paper, pencils

1.   Photocopy the sheet opposite.
2.   Join the number 1's with a pencil, then the number 2's, then the number 3's.

Rhyme: Said the spider to the fly,
"Won't you come and see me.
I'll trap you in my web,
And eat you for my tea!"

(Janet Adams)

Activity: Use the same sheet printed onto card and punch holes on the dots.
Thread the sheet using black cotton or thin wool.

Talk About: If possible, look at a real spider's web. If not, find pictures of web's which are particularly beautiful with water droplets on them.
Look at shapes in a web.
Talk about how strong they are and what they are used for.

© **Topical Resources.** May be photocopied for classroom use only.

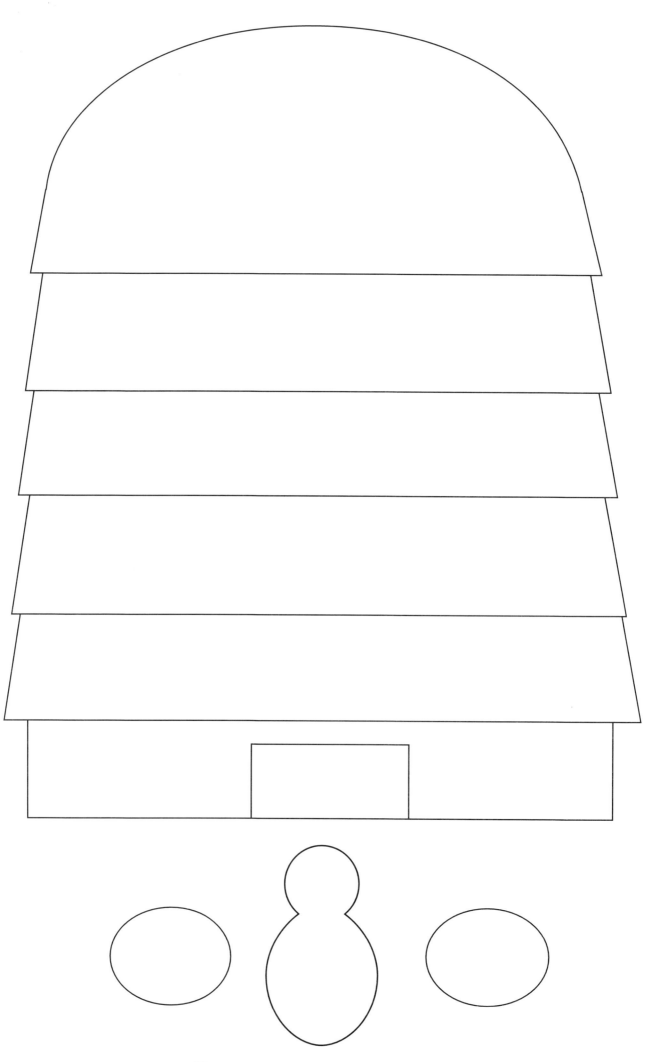

© **Topical Resources.** May be photocopied for classroom use only.

Bees in a Hive

Make: <u>Bees in a Hive</u>

Paper, wax crayons, black paper, greaseproof or tissue paper, glue, scissors, yellow pieces of gummed paper.

1.   Photocopy the beehive.
2.   Cut out five little bees from the pattern opposite out of black paper.
3.   Stick thin yellow stripes onto the bees' bodies.
4.   Make little pairs of wings for each bee out of greaseproof / tissue paper.
5.   Crayon the beehive and the background (unless the hive is going to be cut out).
6.   The five bees can be all stuck onto the hive or Blu Tack can be used so that the bees can be added to the hive as the song is sung.

Rhyme: This is the beehive,
Where are the bees?
Hidden away where nobody sees.
Out of the hive, out come the bees,
1, 2, 3, 4, 5.
(Traditional)

Activity: Cover a small card roll with black sugar paper and stick a disc of black paper over one end. Stick on some yellow gummed strips around the tube. Make some wings from cellophane and stick on to the top of the body. Stick on some eyes on the front (or a pair of wobbly eyes). Suspend from a piece of thin elastic. Use as part of a large display e.g. gardens / outside / summer etc.

Talk About: Honey.
Taste honey.
The work of a bee keeper.
The work of a bee.

42

© **Topical Resources.** May be photocopied for classroom use only.

A Butterfly

Make: <u>A Butterfly</u>

Tissue paper scraps, P.V.A glue.

1. Photocopy or make templates of the shape opposite.
2. Doing a section at a time, cover with P.V.A. glue. Stick on small pieces of coloured tissue paper so that they overlap.
3. When all the surface is covered with paper, cover with a thin layer of diluted P.V.A. Leave to dry completely.

To make 3D, cut out a butterfly shape slightly smaller. Cover with tissue as before and leave to dry completely.
Attach the smaller butterfly to the larger one along the body so that the wings stick out or, two butterflies the same size can be stuck back to back to colour both sides.

Rhyme: Egg to caterpillar,
Then to pupa.
Change to butterfly
Supa dupa!
(Janet Adams)

Activity: Use the same picture photocopied onto card, punch an even number of holes around the edge and use as a threading card.

Talk About: The lovely colours and patterns on a butterfly's wings.
Look at pictures of butterflies.
Compare the caterpillar to a butterfly and talk about the life cycle.
A visit to a Butterfly House.

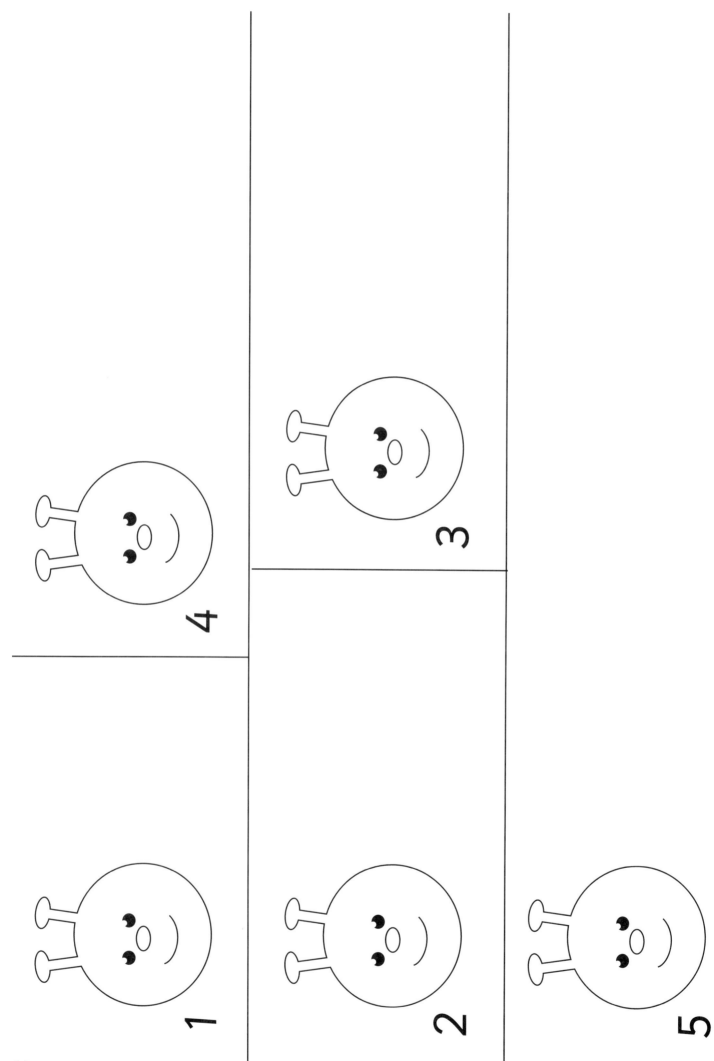

44

© **Topical Resources.** May be photocopied for classroom use only.

Counting Caterpillars

Make: <u>Caterpillars</u>

Small potatoes, small round sponges, green paint

1. Photocopy the sheet opposite.
2. Use potato or sponges to print the right number of circular portions to each caterpillar's body.
3. Draw on little legs.

Rhyme: I'm a little caterpillar,
Furry and brown.
I live in the garden,
And wriggle around.
Put me in your hand,
And soon you'll see.
I'll roll into a ball,
So you can't see me.

(Heather Bell)

Activity: Using an egg tray cut out rows of egg 'portions'. Paint with thick green paint. Stick on two eyes at the front when dry. Thread small pieces of black pipe cleaner through the lower part of the body to make legs.

Talk About: The way caterpillars move.
Other creatures that move like caterpillars.
Go on an insect hunt outside - look under stones, on leaves, on flowers etc.
Try to identify some of the insects.

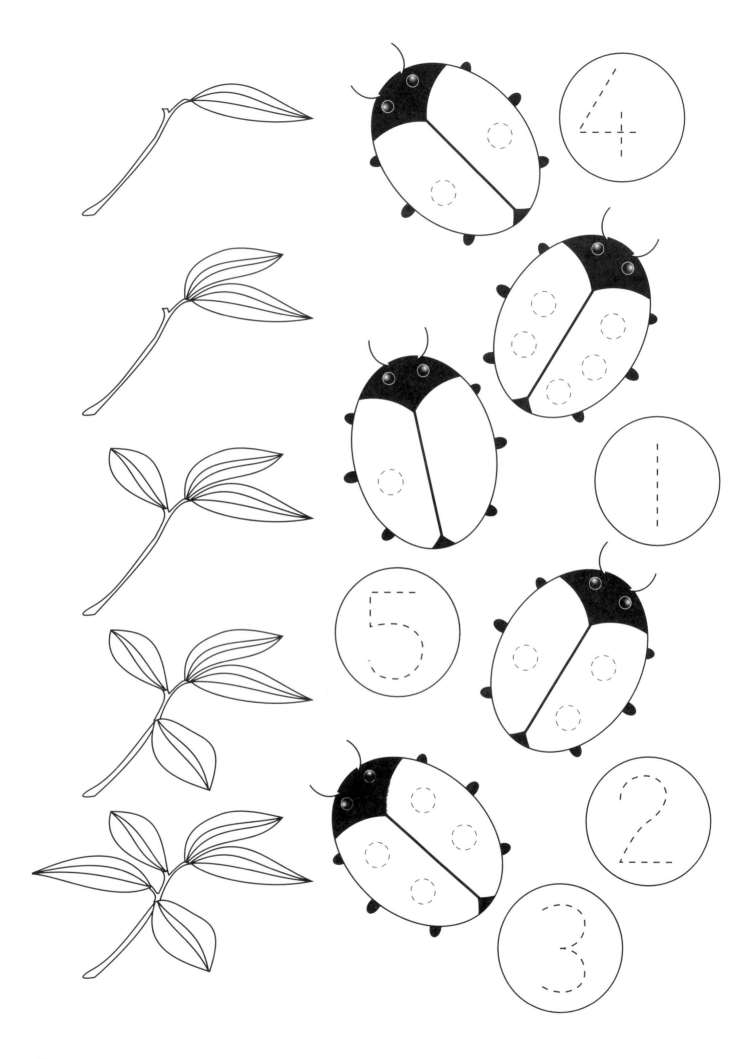

© **Topical Resources.** May be photocopied for classroom use only.

Ladybirds

Make: <u>Ladybirds</u>

Pencils, crayons.

1. Photocopy the sheet opposite for each child.
2. Colour each leaf.
3. Join the dots for each number.
4. Join the numbers to the right little branch.
5. Join the dots to make the spots on each ladybird.
6. Join the right ladybird to the same number.
7. Colour the ladybirds.

Rhyme: Make up a tongue twister about ladybirds e.g.
Lots of little ladybirds land on leaves, looking for a lovely lunch.

Activity: Make a Creepy Crawly Counting Book. Photocopy the following three pages. Cut each page into two. Staple together to make a six page book. The child can illustrate the book.

Talk About: The book "The Bad Tempered Ladybird" by Eric Carle. Whilst looking at the story show the different times on a large clock.
Where Ladybirds can be found.
The time of year Ladybirds are found.
Where Ladybirds keep their wings.

My Creepy Crawly Counting Book

by _____

 ----

one spider

 © **Topical Resources.** May be photocopied for classroom use only.

two ladybirds

2 2 2 2 2 2

✂ ───────────────────────────────

three bees

3 3 3 3 3 3

Ⓒ **Topical Resources.** May be photocopied for classroom use only.

four caterpillars

4 4 4 4 4 4

✂ ——————————————————————————

five butterflies

5 5 5 5 5 5

© **Topical Resources.** May be photocopied for classroom use only.

Looking After Myself

apples

carrots

beans

cake

eggs

fizzy drinks

chips

milk

sweets

cheese

biscuits

chocolate

© **Topical Resources.** May be photocopied for classroom use only.

A Healthy Diet

Make: <u>A Healthy Diet</u>

A4 paper, A3 paper, crayons, scissors, glue

1. Photocopy the sheet opposite, two copies per child.
2. Colour the pictures on one of the sheets.
3. Carefully cut them out.
4. On an A3 sheet of paper carefully draw a line down the middle.
5. On one half of the paper write:
   ✓   I should try to eat lots of ...
   and on the other half write:
   ✗   I should try not to eat lots of ...
6. Talk about the pictures and sort them into two groups. Stick them under the correct headings.
7. Colour and cut out the second sheet of pictures.
8. On a second piece of A3 paper write two headings:
   I like....   I do not like ...
9. Let the children sort out the pictures into the two groups and stick them under the two headings.
10. Compare the two finished sheets. Are the foods we like the healthy ones?

This idea can be used with a group. The small pictures can be enlarged, stuck on to card, laminated then stuck onto larger charts.

Rhyme: Munch, munch, crunch, crunch,
Eat an apple for your lunch!

(Janet Adams)

Activity: Let each child make a healthy fruit salad. Use a plastic knife to cut up pieces of e.g. red apple, green apple, seedless grapes, banana etc. Put in small margarine tubs. Cover the fruit with apple juice. The children can draw a picture of their fruit salad and then eat it.

Talk About: The foods which help bodies grow strong and healthy.
Foods which protect our bodies from illnesses.
Those which in excess will make us overweight and make our teeth go bad.

duck		
sponge		
towel		
soap		
bath		

© **Topical Resources.** May be photocopied for classroom use only.

Keeping Myself Clean Game

Make: <u>**Keeping Myself Clean Game**</u>

A4 card / paper, crayons, scissors

1.   Photocopy the sheet opposite on to paper or thin card.
2.   Colour the pictures.
3.   Cut out the words and pictures. Use as a matching game or it can be made into a lotto game or snap.

Rhyme: Wash these dirty hands,
Wash these dirty hands,
With a scrub a dub a dub,
And a scrub a dub a dub,
Wash these dirty hands.

face, hair, ears, tummy, back, toes etc.
(Traditional)

Activity: What cleans our hands the best?
Dirty four or five children's hands e.g. with paint / soil etc.
Allow to dry on hands.
Test which is the best cleaning agent.
1.   Soap and water.
2.   Wet wipes.
3   Just water.
4.   Bubble bath.
5.   A dry cloth etc.
Talk about what they have found out.

Talk About: What do we use to keep ourselves clean?
Why do we need to keep clean?
Importance of washing hands properly before eating meals, after going to the toilet etc.
Pictures of soap, bubble bath etc. with a display of empty containers.

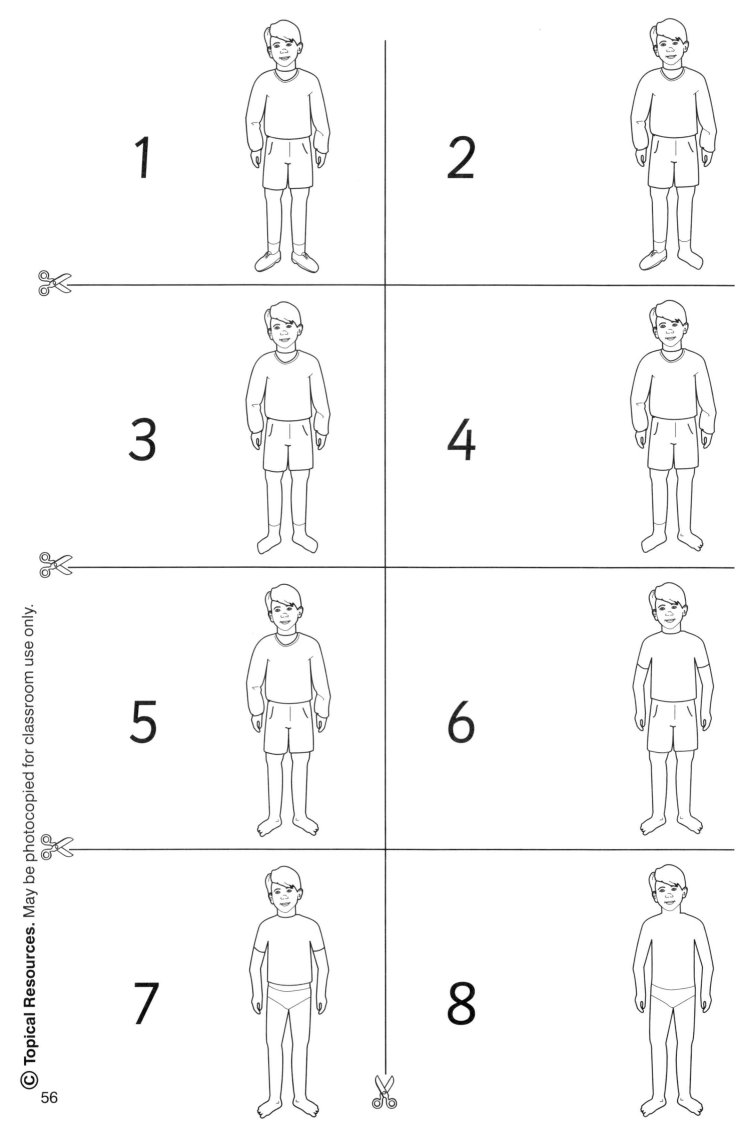

© **Topical Resources**. May be photocopied for classroom use only.

A Getting Dressed Book

Make: <u>**A Getting Dressed Book**</u>

A4 card, crayons, stapler, scissors.

1. Photocopy the sheet opposite on thin card.
2. Colour carefully. Keep the same colour for the same item in each picture e.g. red jumper, blue trousers etc.
3. Cut out and place in order.
4. Staple on the left hand side. As the pages are flicked from the back page, the child will appear to get dressed.

The same picture could be enlarged to make a large frieze with suitable captions.

Rhyme:

This is the way I put on my_____,
Put on my _____,
Put on my _____'
This is the way I put on my _____,
When I get up in the morning.

Pants, shirt, trousers, jumper, socks, shoes etc.

(Janet Adams)

Activity: Each child dresses in shorts, T-shirt and bare feet. Have own clothes in a pile in front. Throw a dice e.g. 1=trousers, 2=jumper, 3=socks, 4=shoes, 5=coat, 6=hat. The first one to get dressed correctly is the winner.

Talk About: The order of putting clothes on.
Practice dressing dolls and teddies and folding up clothes to keep our clothes tidy.
Clothes for different jobs and different weather.
Favourite clothes.

I use

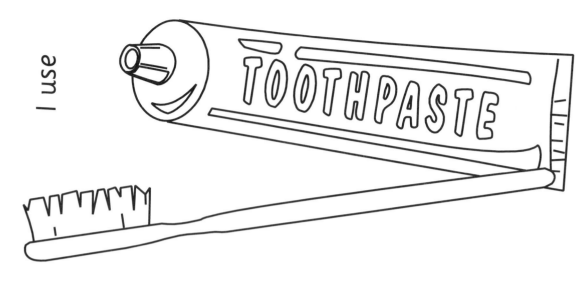

TOOTHPASTE

to clean my teeth

	Morning	Night
Sunday		
Monday		
Tuesday		
Wednesday		
Thursday		
Friday		
Saturday		

© **Topical Resources.** May be photocopied for classroom use only.

A Teeth Cleaning Chart

Make: <u>A Teeth Cleaning Chart.</u>

A4 card, red card, self adhesive coloured spots.

1. Photocopy the sheet opposite.
2. Talk about the chart and colour the large toothbrush and toothpaste (laminate if possible).
3. Send chart home and each time teeth are brushed mark with a tick or coloured spot.
4. Return the charts after an agreed time and talk about the results. If small spots are used the chart can be used for a month at a time.

Rhyme: This is the way I clean my teeth,
Clean my teeth, clean my teeth.
This is the way I clean my teeth,
Every night and morning.

I squeeze my toothpaste on my brush etc.

I move my toothbrush up and down etc.

(Janet Adams)

Activity: Look for pictures in magazines of teeth - animals and humans.
Look for pictures of toothbrushes, toothpaste, mouthwash, dental floss etc.
Make own little scrap book "Taking care of teeth."

Talk About: How to use a toothbrush properly.
How often should we clean our teeth, visit the dentist.
Food for healthy teeth.
If possible invite a dentist to talk to the children.

When the clock says

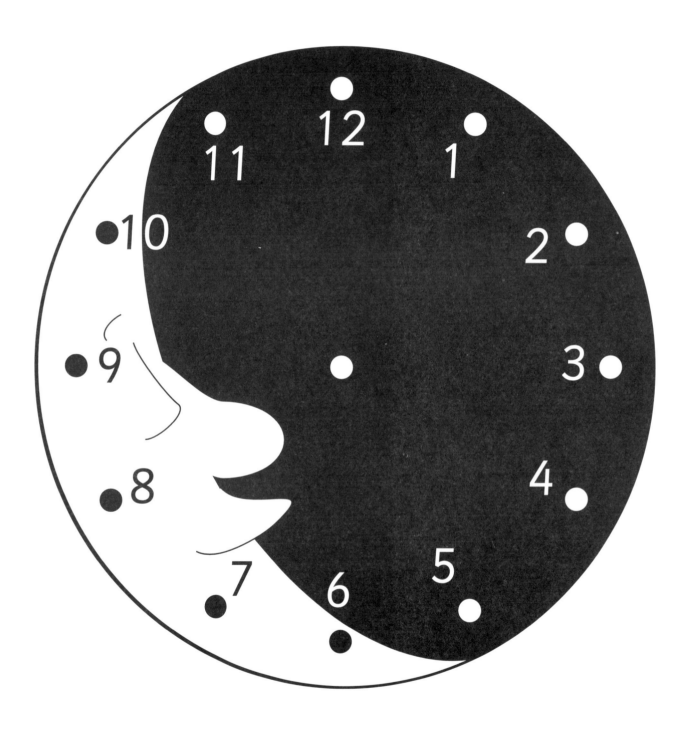

it is bedtime

© **Topical Resources.** May be photocopied for classroom use only.

A Bedtime Clock Mobile

Make: **A Bedtime Clock Mobile**

A4 card, paper fasteners, silver wax crayons, cotton

1.   Photocopy the sheet opposite onto card or photocopy on to paper then stick on to card.
2.   Cut out the pieces carefully.
3.   Bedtime can be drawn onto the clock or card hands can be attached with a paper fastener in the appropriate position.
4.   Fix cotton between each of the 3 pieces to make a mobile.

Rhyme: Go to bed, it's time to sleep,
Close your eyes and do not peep.
Mum will carefully tuck you in,
Pull your covers round your chin.
Go to bed, it's time to sleep,
Close your eyes and do not peep.

(Janet Adams)

Activity: Paint a picture of teddy bear / toy we take to bed. Cut out and make a large frieze or stick on a large painting of a bed and call it "Our bedtime friends".

Talk About: Bedtime stories or our favourite stories.
Things associated with bedtime - removing clothes, getting ready for bed, having a drink, bathtime, cleaning teeth, a story, a cuddle etc.

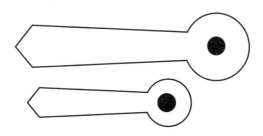

© **Topical Resources.** May be photocopied for classroom use only.

Holding Hands

© **Topical Resources.** May be photocopied for classroom use only.

Holding Hands

Make: <u>Holding Hands</u>

A4 card, coloured card, paper fasteners.

1. Photocopy the sheet opposite or draw round an adult's hand on a piece of card.
2. Draw round a child's hand, cut it out and fix to the bottom of the adult hand with a brass paper fastener.

Make up a phrase of five words to remind the children to hold hands when near a road; point to a finger for each word e.g.

must   hold   mummy's   hand

Rhyme: "Stop" says the red light,
"Go" says the green.
"Wait" says the amber light,
Winking in between.
(Traditional)

Activity: Use two circular lids: e.g. from margarine, cheese portions etc. Paint / colour one red and the other green. Fix each to a stick or a straw. Or make just one lollipop green on one side and red on the other. Play Stop /Go games using the lollipops.

Talk About: Taking care on the roads, walking on pavements, using crossings and how important it is to hold hands.
Importance of looking and listening.
Practice road safety inside before trying it outside in a safe place e.g. (playground).
Use a mirror to make one hand look like two. Now try the activities on the next page.

My Little Mirror Matching Book

by _____

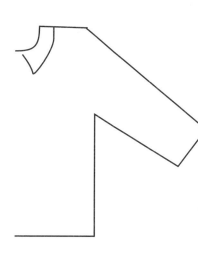

Use a mirror to
make a jacket

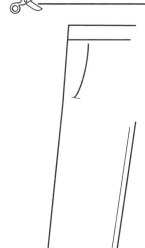

Use a mirror to make a pair
of trousers

Use a mirror to
make a shoe

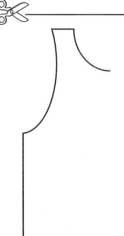

Use a mirror to
make a vest

Use a mirror to
make a face

64

© Topical Resources. May be photocopied for classroom use only.